THIS BOOK BELONGS TO:

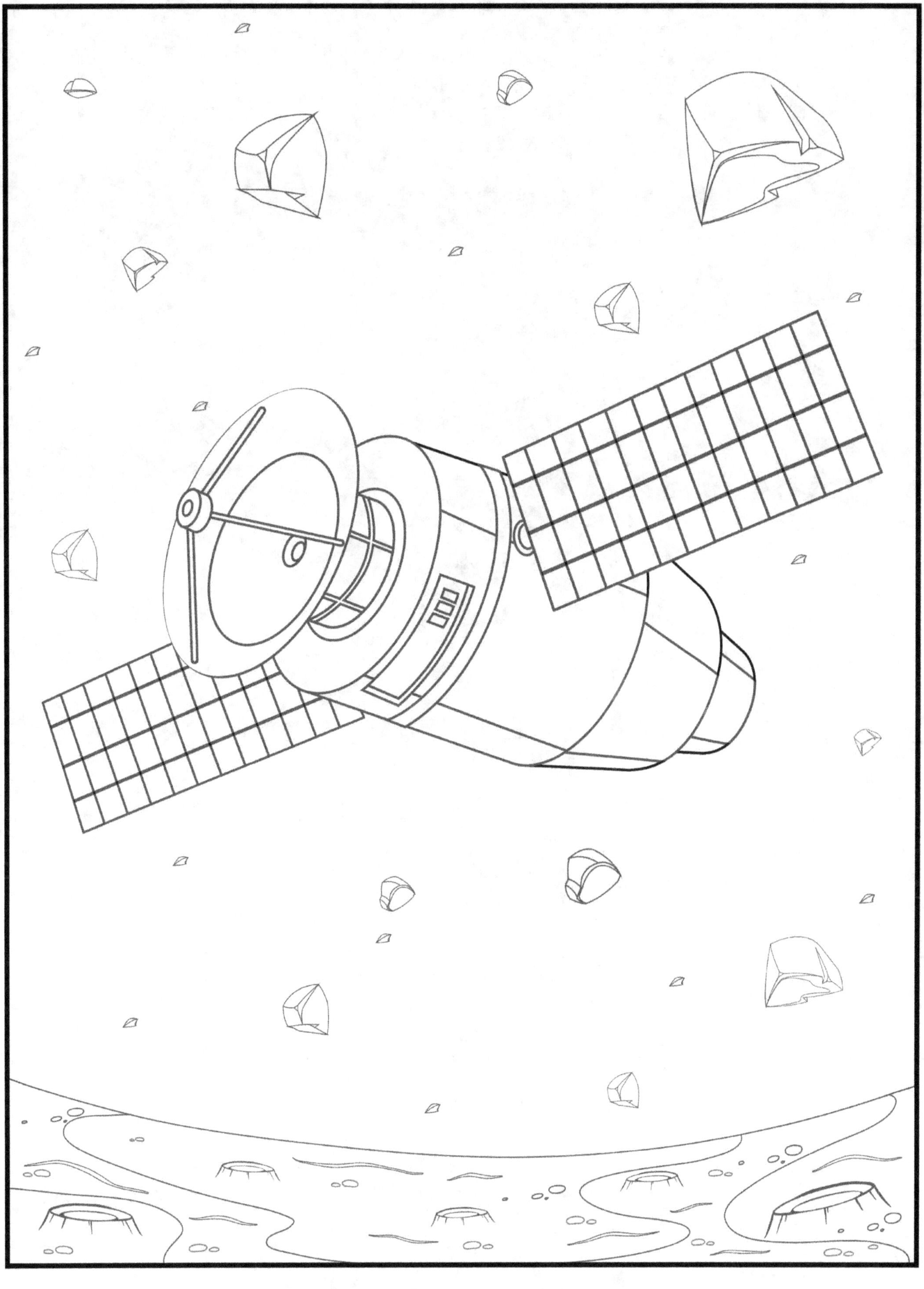

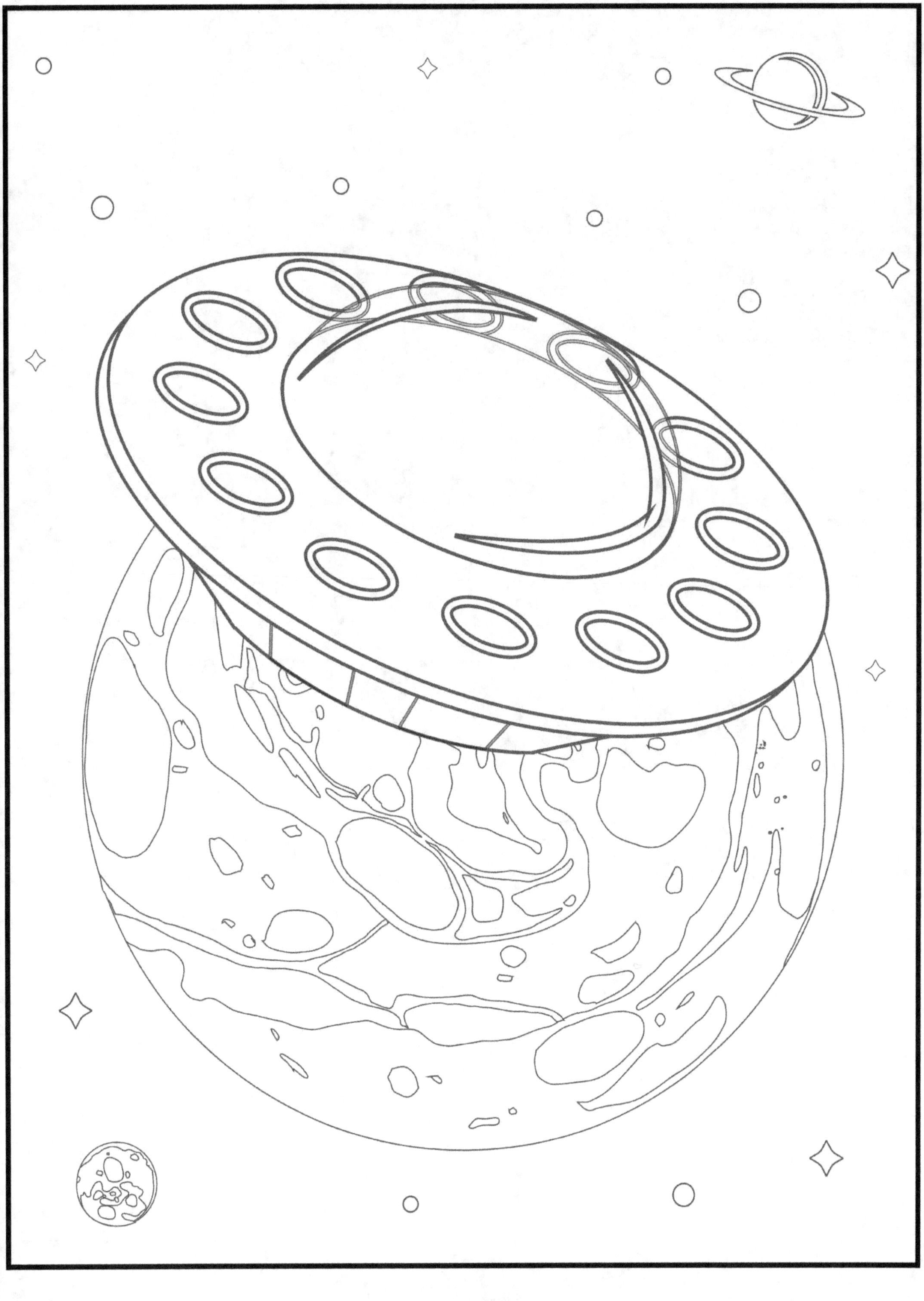

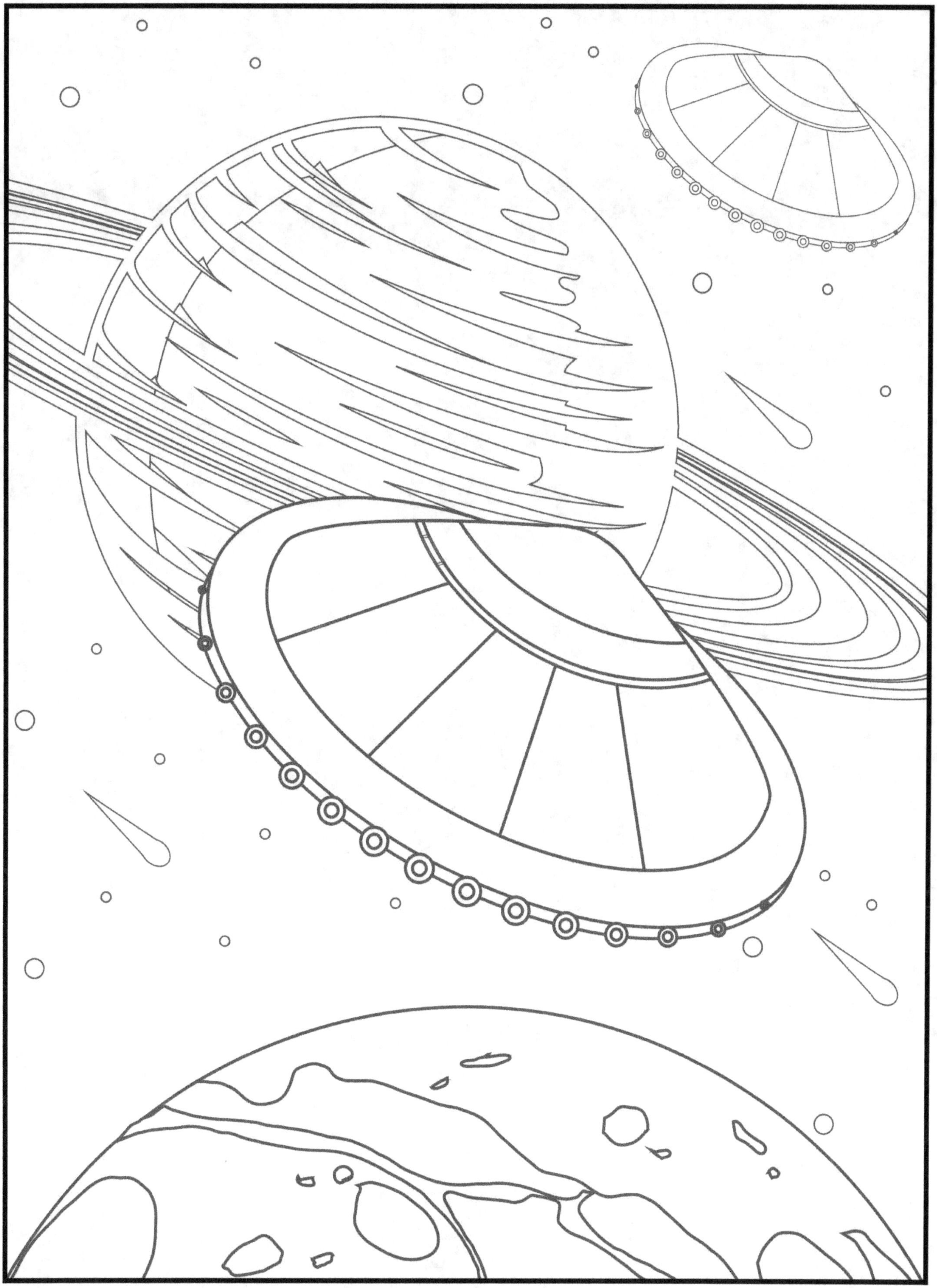

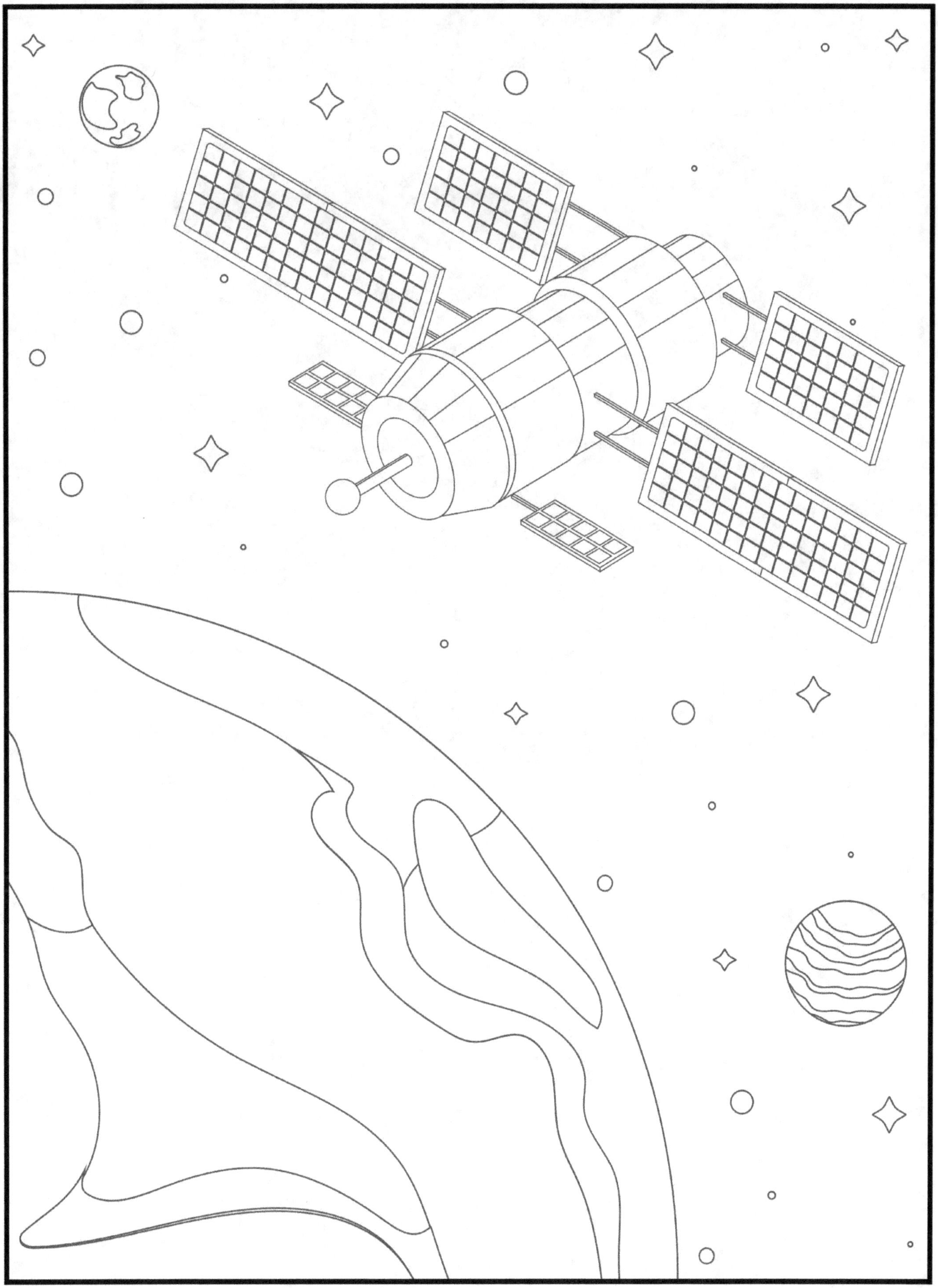

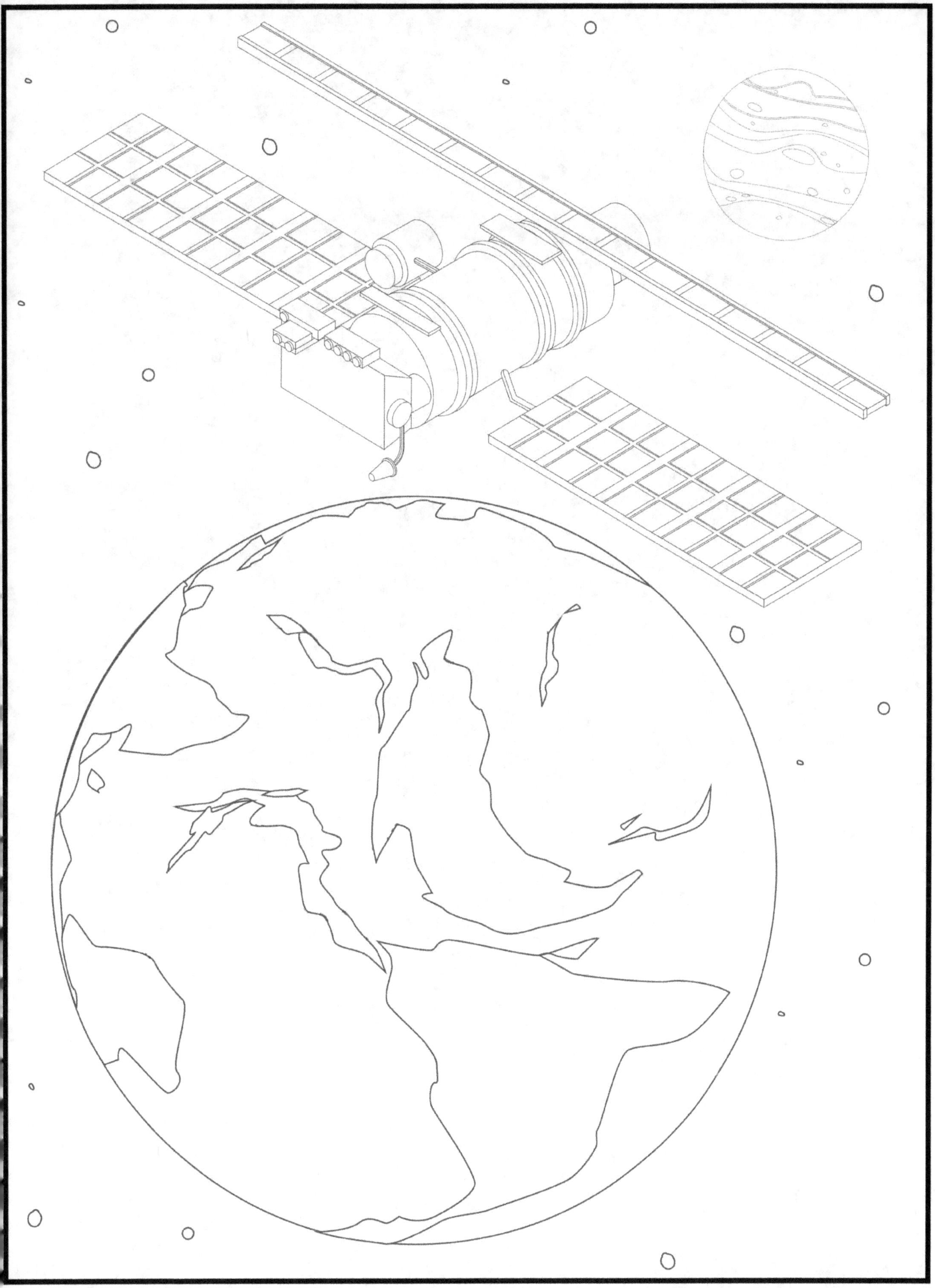

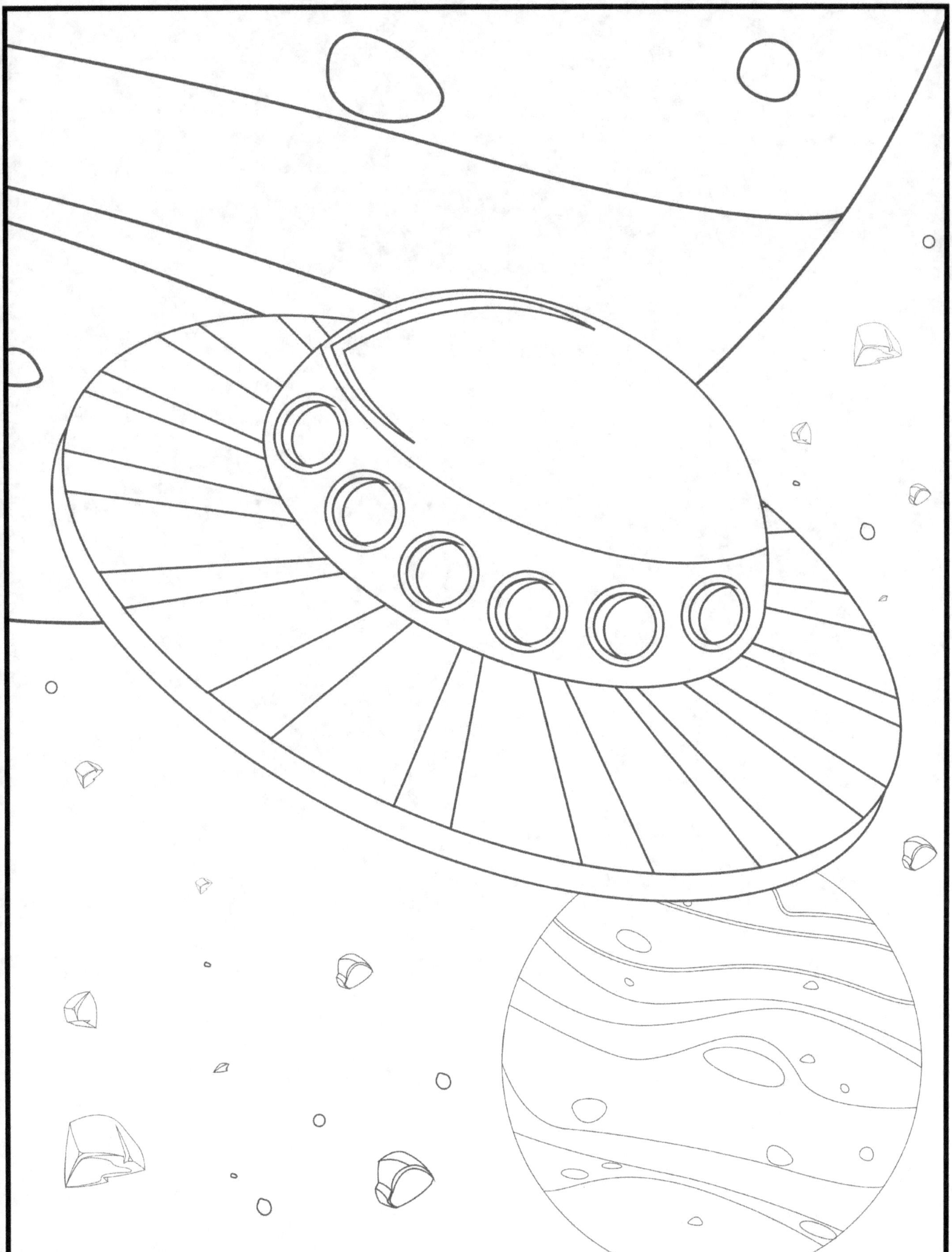

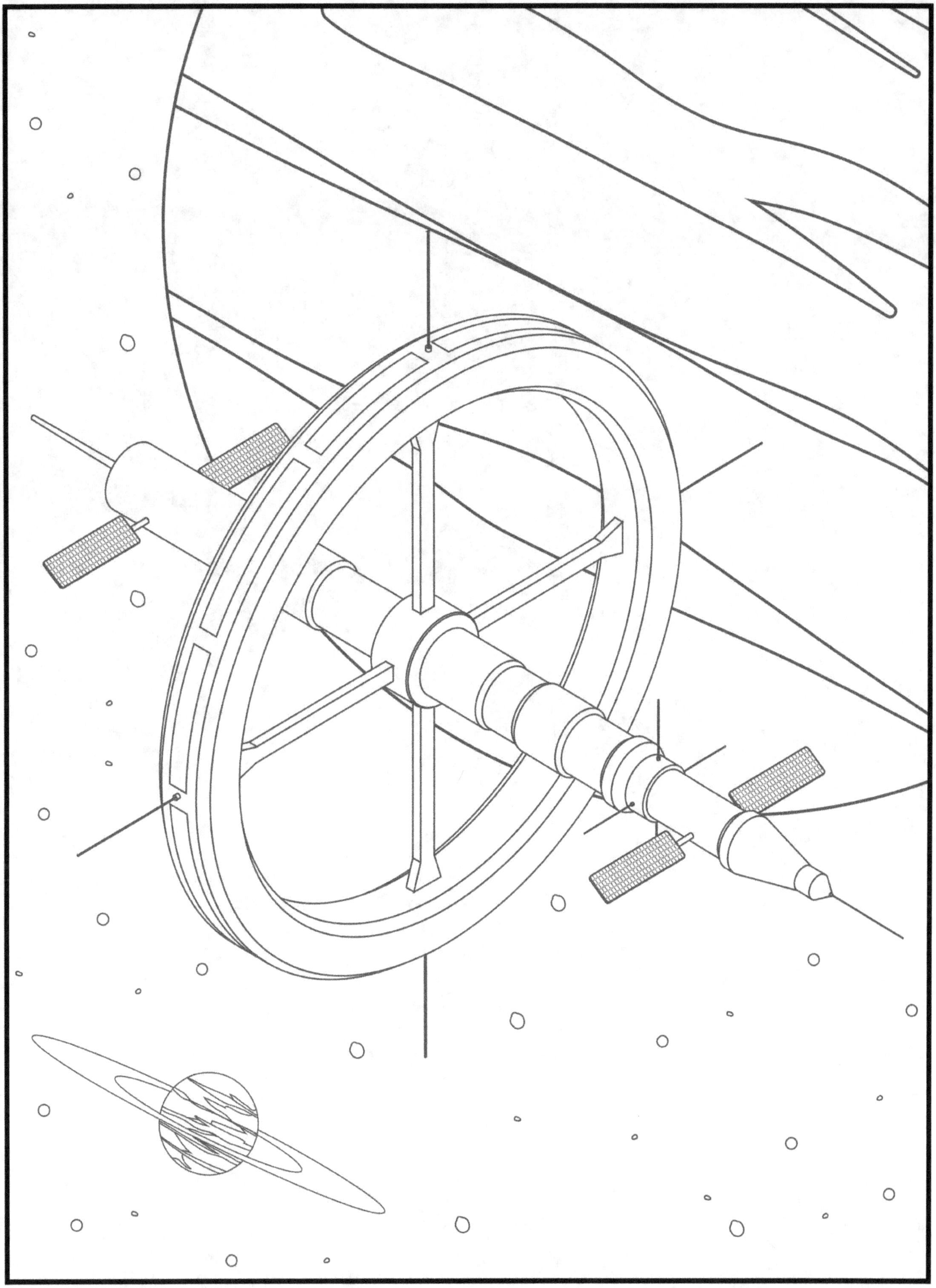

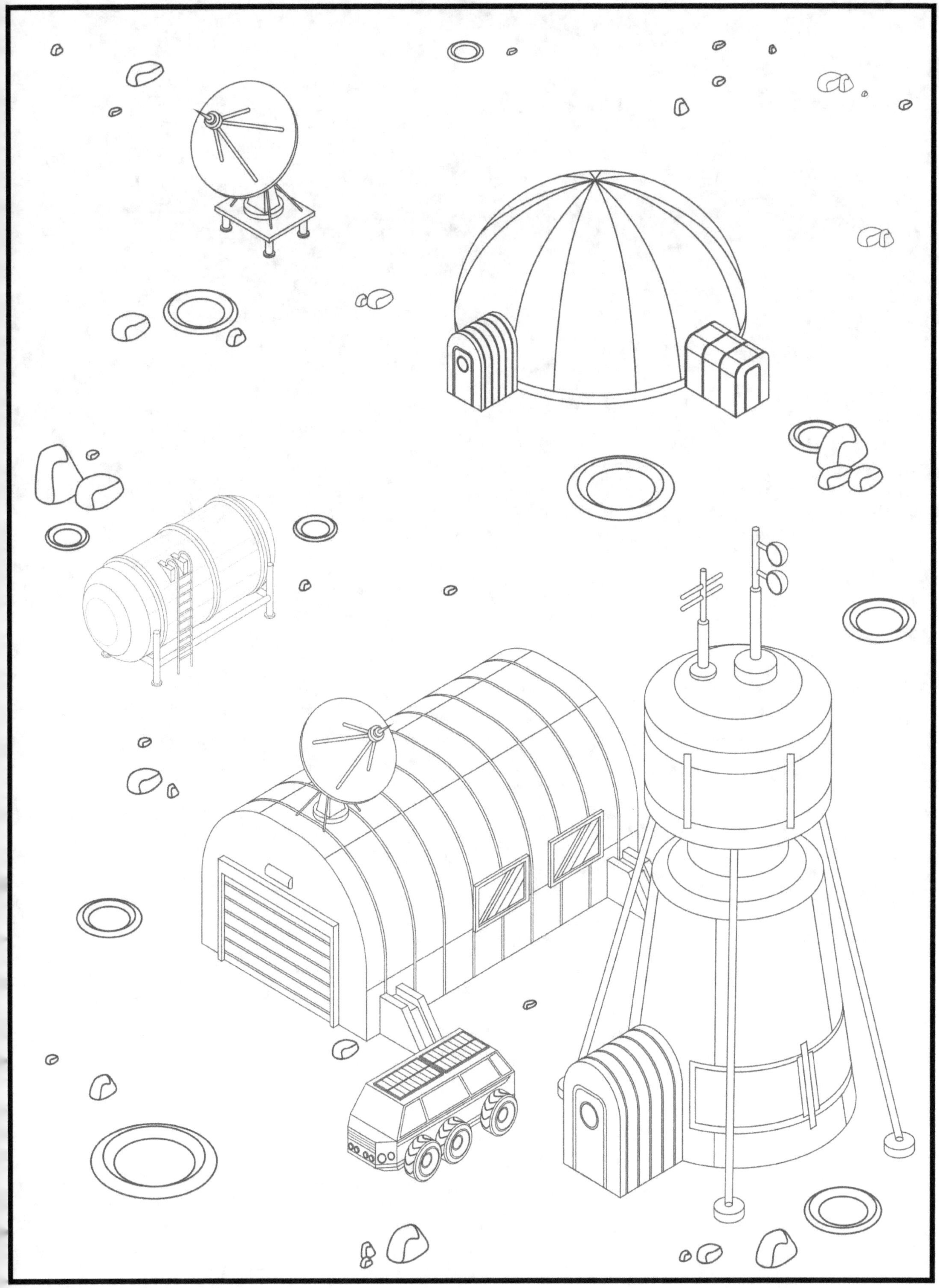

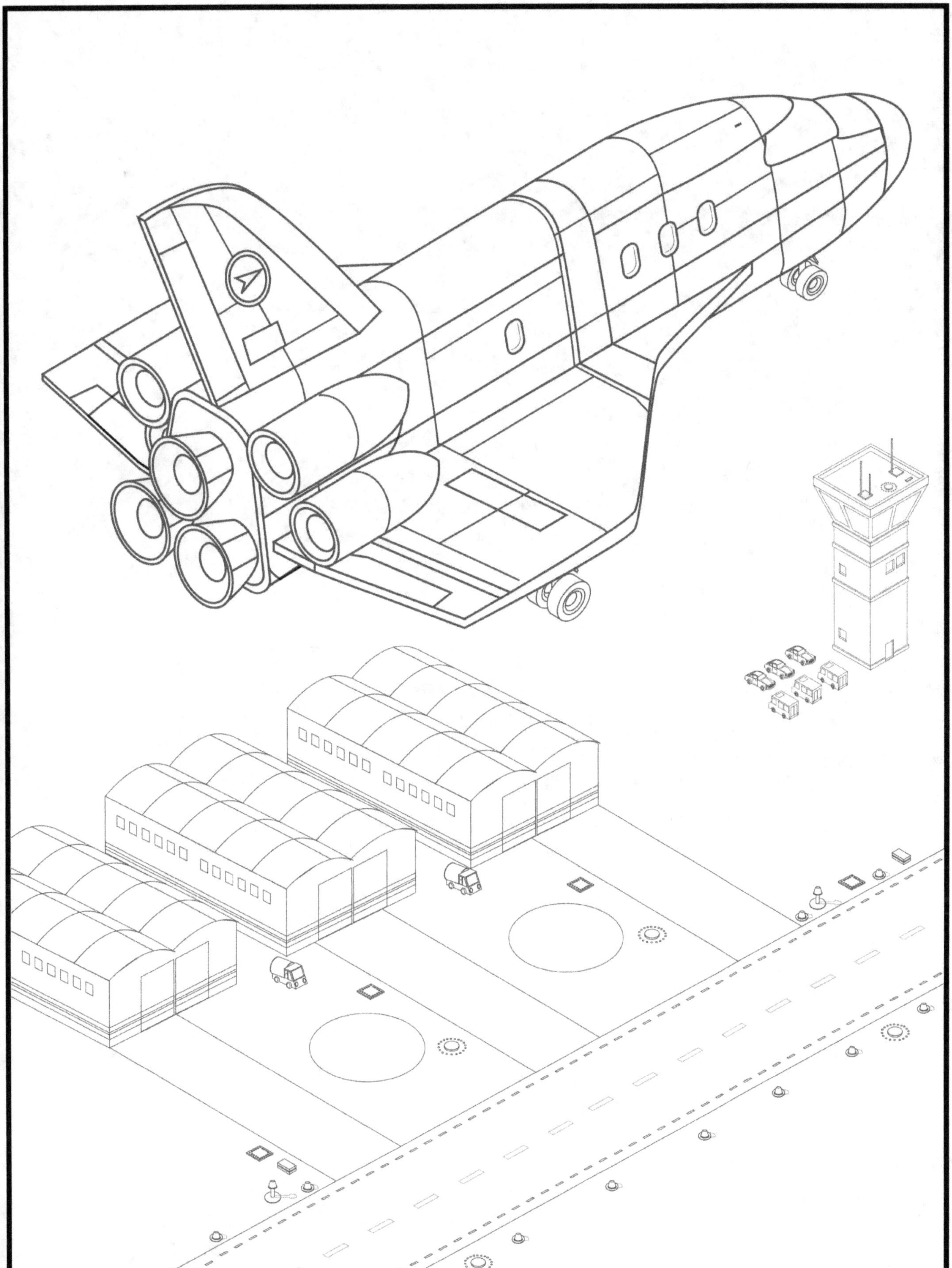

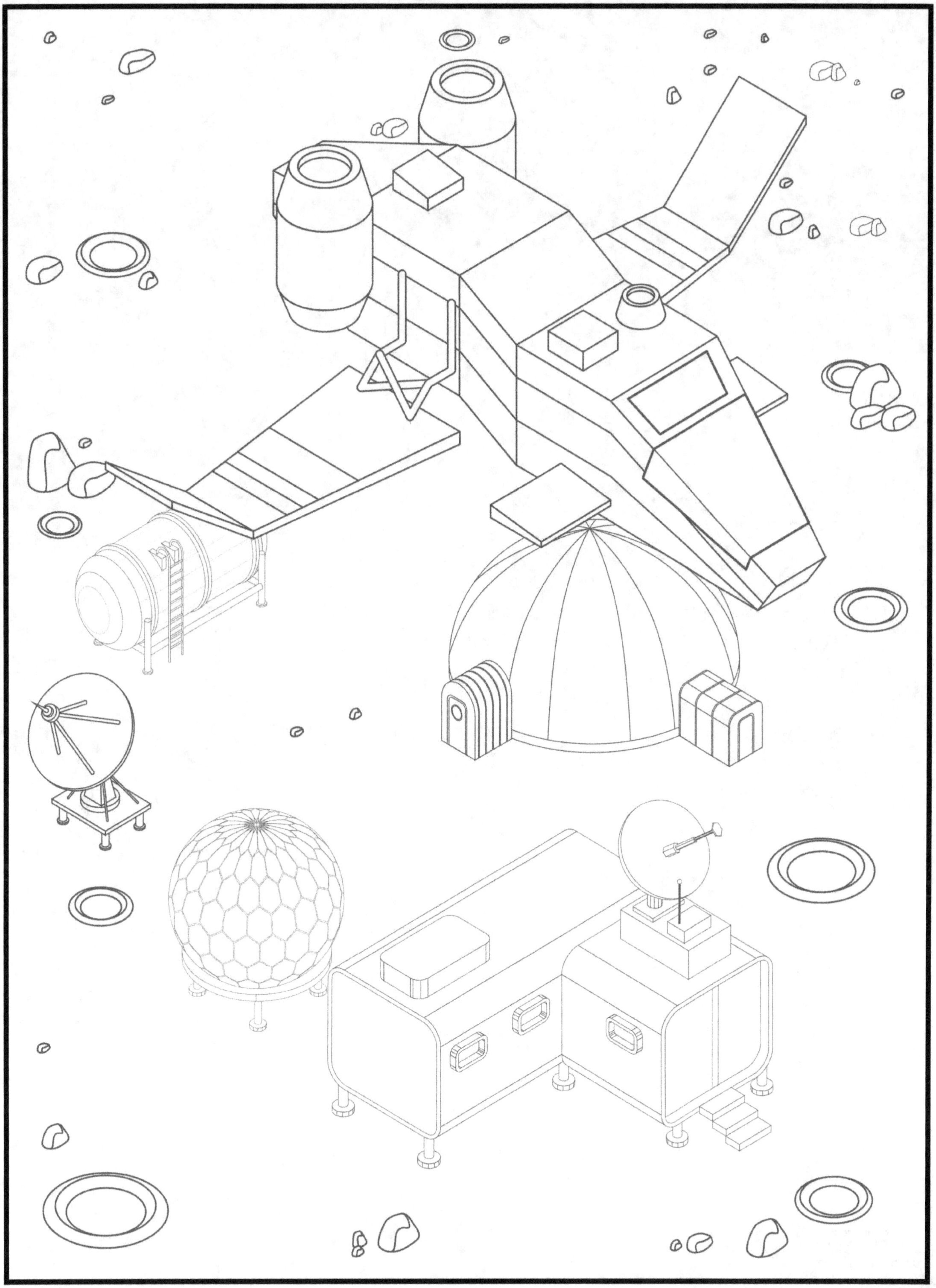

www.ingramcontent.com/pod-product-compliance
Lightning Source LLC
Chambersburg PA
CBHW081534220526
45467CB00010B/3183